The Father's Such

William Epps Mahiri

Order this book online at www.trafford.com
or email orders@trafford.com

Most Trafford titles are also available at major online book retailers.

Print information available on the last page.

ISBN: 978-1-5539-5435-4 (sc)

Trafford rev. 10/26/2020

 www.trafford.com
North America & international
toll-free: 844-688-6899 (USA & Canada)
fax: 812 355 4082

The Father's Such

Dedication

This book is dedicated to my wife Sherrilyn whose faith and confidence in me have inspired me to write for God's glory. Without her love and friendship, this book would yet be a desire of my heart and without substance. It is with much gladness of heart that I dedicate this book to her. God bless you my beloved.

PS.   I would further like to thank those who read and critiqued this work. It is with much work and patience that they have sown to me. May God bless you richly.

FORWARD BY

By LaFayette Scales
Rhema Christian Center
Columbus, Ohio

Many Principals are being released in the Kingdom concerning our life in the presence of God. Thanksgiving, praise and worship are terms that the Spirit of God has unfolded, revealed and opened during this season. Thanksgiving is a response to His greatness. Worship is a response to His Holiness. Ministering priests are acquainted with these terms and practices. Our ministry is what we do but our character is who we are. God deserves desires and expects our Thanksgiving, praise and worship. God will also produce, qualify and develop the character of His ministering Priest.

God is a Spirit. The time has come for true worshippers to worship the Father in spirit and truth for the Father seeketh *SUCH* to worship Him. True worshippers are faithful priests and ministering priests who are consistently dependable in their character, judgments, performance and results. God is preparing His people to move from the event of worship to the process of character development. He is moving from a service of worship to a lifestyle in Him. He will locate, discover and endeavor to obtain and reach *SUCH* to worship Him. He is on a hunt, quest and search to discover, develop, quality and enjoy *SUCH* to worship Him.

Table of Contents

INTRODUCTION

Over the years as the minister of the Lord, it has been my desire, to see the word of God penetrate the very soul and spirit of men and women everywhere. Not that, as the Word of God is preached, they merely hear a good word; but that they would receive it into their hearts and it become life changing. There are those times when we need the Word of God to become a hammer to our circumstances and conditions. We need the strength and the power of Gods truth, to bring deliverance to us in our concerns. Not only is Gods word like a hammer, but also it is as fire that breaketh the rocks in pieces. Jer. 23:29. The strength of who God is then becomes the point of focus in our book. It is not only who he is, but who is he to us? Who is he then in the lives of men? His word establishes the identity of his person: that word in us identifies us in him and with him. There is then the question of men and their identity. Every man/woman from the time of his birth searches for his/her place in the scheme of things. Being the product of the fifties and sixties, (**early youth**) I begin to see tremendous changes in focus and attitudes for a nation, (this nation), and people. There was a cry being made in the streets and on every corner. Counter cultures were emerging in many areas, because of the dissatisfaction of men with the questions of who am I, and where do I belong? What is my purpose for being here? The pursuit of acceptance and approval became the quest of those without any clear moral discipline, mainly because of the hypocrisies of a society estranged from God. This is further born out in each generation, and especially evidenced in the punk rock and gang cultures of this day. Hence we hear a cry being made in the land for the ills of an entire society. Drugs, perversions, scandal, hatreds, and other woes that plague this nation and the world are the burdens, which face us. People are looking for the solution to the problems that are increasingly present. Many of our families are distraught with the hurts and pains, or troubles, which are endemic to many households. Many broken families exist and the single parent is the norm rather than the exception. Our children are hurting and face overwhelming challenges to ever mutating circumstances and conditions. These conditions are not only natural physical problems; (**Aids, Ebola, Cancers, Drugs, etc.,**) but they are direct results of spiritual degenerations, and moral ambivalence.

What is the answer to these troubles men face in their lives? It is my determination that everything in life is predicated on who we are in Jesus Christ. Those who don't know Christ then have nothing upon which to build that is lasting or significant. We who know, Him or rather are known of Him; (Gal. 4:9a), must adapt to the will and purpose of Christ. In this then, we find not only our heritage and purpose; but discover the way to complete success, which is both peaceful and eternal. This is the ability that is given to us through the Word of God.

In His Word, we first discover that the essence of everything God said signifies the character of God. It is who He is. He will never do anything contrary to that which is established in His Word. I wish to take the time to emphasize the Word, because of the significance of the character of the God who spoke it. The first thing that we must realize concerning him is that He is immutable. God is not subject to change. This thought is captured in the 13th chapter of Hebrews in the 8th verse. Jesus Christ the same yesterday, today, and forever In the Old Testament this thought is born out in Malachi 3:6; A *"For I am the Lord, I change not therefore ye sons of Jacob are not consumed."* Because of who God is, (**his immutable character**) they were not consumed. God has given his promises to his people and his word will not change. To change His word, would mean a change in his character; but upon his changeless character stands the immutability of his Word.

The next order of concern then in discussing the character of God is to recognize the association of character with not only his word; but His name. Since a man's name is only as good as his word: (**God is greater than men**) The Bible declares to us that the only thing that God has magnified above his name is his Word. Ps. 138:2 For this reason then, Jesus declares; "Till heaven and earth pass, one jot or one tittle shall in no wise pass from the law, till all be fulfilled" Matt. 5:18 With this we begin to realize the peculiarity of the truth of God concerning his people. The immutable God declares his word and is character bound to preserve it. He speaks regarding the relationship He will have with His people and this is the area of our focus for this book: John's gospel chapter 4, verse 23. "But the hour cometh and now is when the true worshipers shall worship the Father in spirit and in truth: for the Father seeketh **SUCH.**" This is the mystery of God revealed in his son and made manifest in the world. It is the giving of Christ to all those who will accept him and the will of the Father for their lives. **SUCH,** who believe and obey the commandments of a sovereign God. Let us seek the truth in this passage of scripture together.

CHAPTER ONE

THE CONFRONTATION
(little gods)

Our first need is to define the word, SUCH which is the basis for this writing.

In the Greek; **Such** is the word **Toioutos,** meaning; truly this, or of this sort, **(it denotes character or individuality)** like as, or such a one. In Philippians 2:25- 30; the Apostle Paul asserts that he found it necessary to send Epaphroditus, whom he termed as his brother and companion in labor, and fellow soldier; but their messenger and he who ministered to Paul's wants; for them. He speaks of the heaviness and longing in the heart of Epaphroditus for the Philippians because they had heard about his sickness. Vs. 26; Paul says then that he (Epaphroditus) had been sick unto death but God had mercy both on Epaphroditus and himself by rising up this man, whom Paul obviously loved and believed dear and precious to himself Vs. 27. The Apostle then assures the Philippians of his carefulness to send Epaphroditus to them, that they may rejoice and that he himself may be less sorrowful Vs. 28. Now, in looking at this scripture, we begin to note that there are unique qualities, which present themselves in the character of Epaphroditus and are clear and obvious to Paul. Paul sends

Epaphroditus because of the love displayed in his desire to see them. It is a reciprocal regard, in as much as they have longed for him in his illness; to see him well. While love is the desire to benefit someone else at the expense of our selves; (not desiring anything in return) Epaphroditus is concerned that they would be distraught at his hurt. In verse 29-30; Paul says; "receive him therefore in the Lord with all gladness; and hold **Such** in reputation, because for the work of Christ, he was nigh unto death, not regarding his life to supply your lack of service toward me." Love is prominent in the relationship that both Paul and Epaphroditus have for each other and for the body of Christ. **The Such** will display the evidence of His character as born out in the Word of God according to Gal. 5:22-25. While it is obvious that the fruit of the Spirit are operating in the Body of Christ at some level; it is equally obvious that they are not working to the extent that God the Father can be perfected in the Church. The Church has operated in carnality and tradition, while being focused on gain and possession. This then, is equated with being righteous and spiritual. While it is the desire of The Lord to give unsearchable riches to the Church; they will be given to a Church that has his heart. They will be given to a people, which imbibe his character. In Ephesians 3; Paul said, "Unto me, who am less than the least of all saints, is this grace given, that I should preach among the Gentiles the unsearchable riches of Christ. One of the qualities of the Spirit of the Lord is that of trustworthiness. It is that place of relationship that God desire to establish in every believer. How can we believe Him whom we can't trust to do what he said he would do?

So then, we find a theme in the Word of God, which is continual in those relationships, which are spoken of regarding the cloud of witnesses of which the bible speaks. (Hebrews chapter 12) When we view chapter 11 of that same book of Hebrews; we find those who have believed God and their sacrifices of faith. The confidence they possessed in the living God is evident in the example of Noah in verse 7. "By faith Noah, being divinely warned of things not yet seen, moved with godly fear, prepared an ark for the saving of his household, by which he condemned the world and became heir of the righteousness which is according to faith." Then; the evidence that we trust him is our ability to believe what he said. God will then try our faith in Him. This too points to the age-old struggle for His approval, which can only come by our faith and obedience to Christ. God is not impressed by the things of men that have man's will as the rule of importance, but by our faith and confidence in the God of all creation. In all, the purpose for which we were created is one of worship and to serve Him. The need in every person to worship is clearly seen in those things we reverence. We place them in the order of their greatest significance to us. It could be our money or our possessions; it could be our attachments to jobs and positions, even education and or training that we have received. These are some of those things which men reverence rather than the God who made them. Here then we realize the need to turn to him with our whole heart in faith and yield to the desire that He has for us as his beloved. What an awesome privilege to be a part of the will of the living God. Only a wise God could hold such a high place of regard for men. (*What is man that thou art mindful of him Heb. 2:6*) It is God who has chosen us in him before the foundation of the world. We as the chosen must learn to submit with our whole heart to the desires of the One who has chosen us. Oftentimes, there is a struggle for peace in our hearts and minds to grasp the truth when we only need to do the truth. While Jesus said in John's gospel; *"ye shall know the truth and the truth shall make you free;"* (*John 8:32*) it is also apparent that we must first believe that the Word of God is absolutely true and accept its veracity. With this then we see that the main problem for men is that of control what He said in order to justify our thoughts and desires. When I accept the Word of God as the absolute rule for my living; I can walk in agreement and wait for the revelation. **(we know in part)** *1 Cor.13:9*

Jesus then, as the main character of the scripture, is set forth in the time of his visitation, to bring not only salvation and deliverance to the world; but to confront in many instances, the religious order of that day. The confrontations that follow his ministry are results of the rudiments of men. They are commandments that have come into being through the will of the flesh; rather than the will of God. Jesus in contending with the Scribes and Pharisees said; *"Well hath Esaias prophesied of you hypocrites, as it is written, this people honoureth me with their lips, but their heart is far from me"* *Mark 7:6.* In this, the stage is set for the gathering of a people established in faith and complete obedience to the will of the Living God. The prevailing attitude of the religious order of that day was a pseudo-righteousness that was exterior to the true righteousness of God. They cared about the things which had nothing to do with God's heart and desire for them as a people: Things such as eating with unwashed hands, eating and drinking with publicans and Christ's regard for the lowly. These things they felt were beneath them and they set themselves as little gods over the people. This prompts Jesus to call them hypocrites, because they rejected the commandments of God to keep and enforce their traditions. This kind of deference to the word of God is yet evident in our day. Many place a weightier importance upon the wisdom of men and have rejected the wisdom of the Holy Spirit. A further deception is the belief of those who continue in the traditions and rudiments of men; that what they were taught is in fact the will of God. (***It is a spiritual and moral assurance, that if what we have been taught and believe does not measure up with the character of God; it is not true and should be dismissed as the rule of our will and living.***) When Jesus began to minister in the power of the Spirit, they *(the religious order)* found themselves challenged with the truth of God. We are living in a similar hour; where men are being challenged and have even been affrighted of the move of God. There is an eruption of the Holy Spirit in the earth and revelation knowledge in the word of God is pulling down traditions and breaking the yokes of bondage, which have held the people of God, captive. Men are moving into a new realm of experience and relationship in the Holy Spirit. Even as the religious order of Jesus' time was intimidated by the drawing away of the masses from the traditional to that which was righteous in God and spiritual: so now there is a drawing away of the people into a bold new place in Christ. The bible declares of the people, that; *"they were astonished at his doctrine: for he taught them as one having authority, and not as the scribes."* Lu. 7:29; They were again intimidated, because of his commands to forgive unconditionally and to love without reservation. It was foreign to the religious world.

Now, Jesus was persecuted by the order of that day, because he was not one of them. He did not cater to the philosophies and theologies, nor to the man made, men imposed, ritualistic; behaviors of the scribes and pharisees. They were set at variance, because of their sins. Jesus exposed them by speaking the truth. The truth exposes everyone with no disposition to do otherwise. In this day and hour, the ritualistic, spirit of the scribes and pharisees has been manifest in the churches. This type of confrontation is in the forefront today, of all that Christ has purposed to do in the Church. God is raising up a people that will have his character; that will not take under for the sake of appeasing the desires of men. They will be a people with one heart and a desire; to please the God who called them. They will preach His Word and love the unlovely. They will press through into the purposes of the Father; by prayer and great intercession. It is a people who will stand up and declare the sovereign might and power of an awe-inspiring God. They will not hide the truth nor will they shun the responsibility laid upon them. Even as Jesus, they will not hesitate to do the ministry they are charged with.

*"**Now when the pharisees of that day heard that Jesus baptized more disciples than John.**"* Jn.4:1; It was distressing to them and they were greatly aggravated over his actions in persuading men with his teachings because he did not fit their patterns and traditions. Jesus was driven to fulfill the purposes of his Father. *(He must needs go through Samaria)* Vs.4 The Church that God is establishing in this end time; is a Church, which possesses an urgency to do the will of and fulfill the purpose of God the Father through Jesus Christ. Whereas Jesus told the disciples; *"I have meat to eat that you know not of. My meat is to do the will of the Father and to finish his work."* Jn.4:32-34 They who will do the will of Christ will eat of the purposes of the God who has called them. It is a hunger and a thirst for the desires of Christ. There is a travail in the Spirit to see the heart of God manifest in the earth. It will not be denied by the hardness of religiosity and men's sanctimony. But, it is a manifestation of the Sons of God with power and demonstration of the Spirit of God; which is irrefutable and unparalleled in scope and power. This is a move of God that will sweep

through this nation and around the world. It is a move that will see the separation of the Old Prophetic Order of leadership in the Church *(the old leadership steeped with tradition and men's commandments)* from the New Prophetic Order *(fearless and undaunted by tradition and opinions of men; energetic to be absolutely obedient to God's Holy Spirit)*. It is a move that will establish a far more spiritually aggressive and warrior like people. *"The kingdom of God suffereth violence, and the violent take it by force."* Matt. 11:12 This is a very violent and aggressive generation of men and women in the natural; who will be saved and changed by Christ, but with a warring mentality to take the things of God and go forth for His glory. Yet there are and have been hindrances to fulfilling the desires of Christ in bringing the Church into its power. Not the least of these hindrances is the unwillingness of the Old Prophetic Order of leadership to press into the Spirit and discover the heart of God. Or having seen the will of God by the Spirit they have been resistant to change because of the desire to placate the sentiments of people. There has even in the Church, been a resistance to the power and anointing of Christ: resistance to tongue talking and gifts of the Spirit in operation. It is primarily because of the lack of teaching and acceptance of the Word of God as sovereign. Men, who without courage to believe and accept Gods Word have walked in disobedience. Because of the natural man's inability to know or interpret the things of God, the Church has lived in partial anointing and victories; even though the word clearly states; *"Nay and we are more than conquerors through him that loved us."* Rom. 8:37 Many have been far more interested in rule and gain than in Gods purpose.

Herein then is the first confrontation by the Spirit of God. It is to bring down strongholds, which have existed in the realm of leadership. The mantle of authority is being passed to a generation of men and women who will obey the God of their righteousness. They who will be relentless in their pursuit of his will. Those of the existing authority who will not come obedient to this move of the Spirit; will die out, much like Israel in the wilderness. Let us take a sidebar to the implications of this. **(not obeying the Spirit of God to be led according to his dictates)** God gave the

Children of Israel the promise of His Word. He did not give it in a vacuum. What he spoke, he is well able to perform. Yet, there is the lack of faith and agreement on the part of Israel to believe and follow after the Word. This happened because they did not mix the Word of God with faith. Then, they wondered in the wilderness. Heb. 4:2b This is the principal of scripture which we must not lose sight of. If we will not believe God, and mix his word with faith; we are destined to wonder in the wilderness i.e. to walk in lack of wisdom and understanding of the purpose and intent for which we were called. Therefore, we become unable to fulfill our destiny. This is not about the things of men, but the things of God. God is bringing change into the earth through the Church. He has always brought wilderness experience to them who will not believe. **(God will not allow those who only know the way of bondage to enter Canaan.)** Men must have a change of heart and be willing to war for their inheritance. They must also allow that God is the sovereign and only wise God. Their faith and confidence must be in Him.

The religious order of this day is not unlike the religious system of that day. It has been overwhelmed by the same spirit that operated then. There were several attitudes, which troubled Moses in his attempt to lead them into the promise. Firstly, we see self-seekers or **(spirit of Korah/Diotrephes);** the desire of other men to have pre-eminence over the people of God. Korah and Dathan along with 250 princes of Israel had gathered themselves together against Moses and Aaron. (Num. 16:1) They challenged the leadership of the congregation and God was wroth. This is a change, which was attempted through rebellion and sedition. The change of God that is coming now will come through the workings of the Holy Spirit in compliance with the will of God. Furthermore, God will resist any attempt on the part of men to intervene with His purpose apart from his character. **(Rebellion is not a part of his character)** There is a major change in character, which is coming to the body of Christ. not that He changed, but that we become more like Him.

Now, the attitude of Diotrephes is one of speaking against the faithful of Christ with malicious words and a refusal to receive the brethren and hindering others from receiving them. He forbade The Word of God and its influence; casting them out of the Church. (3 Jn. 9-10) This spirit then desires to dominate and rule over the things of God and to manipulate them for its own eminence. **(they become little gods)** Jesus in ministering to a blind man is asked the question in John chapter 9:2; *"Who did sin, this man or his parents, that he was born blind."* in verse 3, Jesus answered, *"Neither has this man sinned, nor his parents: but that the works of God should be made manifest in him."* Here Jesus shows the intent of the Father; in that his ministry and purpose should be fulfilled in the opening of the blinded eyes. Christ later chides the leaders for their spiritual blindness, Jn.9:41; *"If ye were blind ye should have no sin; but now ye say, we see; therefore your sin remaineth."* There is blindness to the purposes of God that are manifest in the Church world. They will not allow men to come obedient to the move of the spirit of God. It stems out of their desire to regulate the things of Christ to suit their own desires. *(The traditions of men)* Matt. 15:9 **(little gods)** it is interesting to note that Jesus did not come to reveal the plan of God to the leadership of that day. He goes about to establish the plan and purpose of the Father, by revealing it to the ignorant and unlearned men. In Acts 4:13; Christ is realized in those that were in opposition to his disciples; *"Now when they saw the boldness of Peter and John, and perceived that they were ignorant and unlearned men; they marveled; and they took knowledge of them that they had been with Jesus.)*

Christ was not looking for men who held the traditions of their Fathers: but for men that could be trained in righteousness of the God, to fulfill the commission of God the Father. *"But God hath chosen the foolish things to confound the wise; and God has chosen the weak things of the world to confound the things which are mighty. And the base thins of the world, and the things which are despised, hath God chosen, yea, and things which are not, to bring naught things that are: that no flesh should glory in His presence."* 1Cor. 1:27-29. Men who would be obedient were his choice. They were not chosen for their abilities scholastically, or for their skill in the Word of God; but for their willingness to follow Christ. They did not fit the organizational structure of the day. This would be true as well, in the "New Prophetic

Order. We have not been chosen for our greatness or several abilities but for our willingness to serve obediently. He has called us that we may become an extension of His son in the earth.

Now, the Church is not an organization (**although organized**); but it is an organism that follows the Holy Ghost and is empowered by it. It is motivated by the Holy Ghost and directed according to the desire of God. We are not the Sons of God because we are religious; but because we are led by the Spirit of God. Romans 8:14 states; *"For as many as are led by the Spirit of God, they are the Sons of God."* Often, men are attempting to do the will of God through their own means and abilities. It is not by our education and teaching, nor by our acumen or training, that we will accomplish for Christ. It takes the instruction of Gods word and adherence to the truth to be effective for Christ. *"Ye shall know the truth and the truth shall make you free).* John 8:32. Here in this passage of scripture, there is an acute sense of propriety established by Christ. It is the ability to gain understanding of the revelation given into our spirit by the Holy Spirit. He will teach you all things! The Lord first asserts that: *"If you continue in my word, then are ye my disciples indeed."* Jn 8:31. One of the major troubles facing the New Testament Church is a subtle type of disobedience. It is not the kind, which is a blatant rebellion against the truth, or even the whole will of God. It is an omission: The failure to continue in the Word. It is the failure to walk in the fullness of the revealed truth. Jesus showed the early Church how to walk in His word. The Apostle Peter recorded; *"for even hereunto were ye called: because Christ also suffered for us, leaving an example, that ye should follow his steps."* 1Peter 2:21. At this point it becomes necessary to ask a question. Why has the Church been lacking in its effort to do all that is commanded? I believe that the major reason is as follows. When men begin to walk in the will of Christ, there is a persecution, which comes against them. All those who choose to be obedient to the whole will of Christ will suffer persecution. Many are not ready to suffer for his sake; in performing the purposes of the Living God. Yet, if Christ is our example; then the pattern, and Gods will for us is clear. The Bible tells us that; *"Many are the afflictions of the* *righteous."* Ps. 34:19.   The Apostle Peter said of Jesus; *"Who did not sin, neither was guile found in His mouth: Who when he was reviled, reviled not again; when he suffered, he threatened not: but committed himself to him that judgeth righteously."* 1Peter2:22-23.

Inherent in the desire of Christ in us: comes the responsibility for enduring affliction and suffering. To suffer the persecutions and attacks of the enemy, **(Satan)** and many times be criticized and even ostracized for our obedience to Christ, gives men anxiety and perplexity because they cannot control Him with the will of the flesh. His things require the wisdom of the Spirit to accomplish. It is with this suffering; we learn to commit ourselves to him that judges righteously. These things are endured for the sake of Him that called us and chose us. (*"According as he hath chosen us in Him before the foundation of the world, that we should be holy and without blame before Him in Love."*) Eph.1:4. Even as we have seen in scripture the confrontation of Jesus with the religious order of that day; the much educated; we yet see the same parallel of the Spirit working in this day and hour. This is not an attack against education. Education is very necessary to the growth of the people of God. Whether it is formal or informal training, it is helpful if we remember that we are Spirit led and motivated people. The Apostle Paul said: *"But what things were gain to me, those I counted loss for Christ. Yea doubtless, I count all things but loss for the excellency of the knowledge of Christ Jesus my Lord: for whom I have suffered the loss of all things, and do count them but dung, that I may win Christ. And be found in him not having mine own righteousness, which is of the law, but that which is through the Faith of Christ, the righteousness which is of God by Faith."* Phil.3:7-9. Paul was a very learned and well-versed man in the law. This is a clear indication that he placed no trust in his background as the source and supply for his ministry and his anointing in Christ.   Paul understood that the real worshipers must worship in Spirit and in truth. Jn 4:23. Christ's desire is for the true worshipper to be revealed and the heart of the Father be manifested. This then should compel men to search for his heart rather than the will of the flesh.

Now, it is certain that the ministers of the Lord Jesus Christ will suffer for the giving forth of this type of teaching. It exposes the traditional, sectarian, and denominational prejudices of this day: God will equip the New Prophetic Order with the power and demonstration of the Spirit. This is in keeping with the Word of God to the Church. It will form the very prophetic heart and lips of the Lord Jesus. **(These signs shall follow them that believe.)** In my ministry as an Evangelist prior to being called into Pastoral ministry; I had the occasion to preach revival at a particular church where the pastor had a heart for this prophetic move of God and was receiving much opposition for her vision. During a message that I was preaching and in the heart of the truth that the Lord was giving concerning the cost of receiving the anointing of God; God spoke to my spirit and told me to speak some things he had given me concerning the opposition she was receiving. I was very much pressed to say what I was being given because of the severity of the Word of the Lord which was in my mouth. Nevertheless, I had to speak the Word of the Lord. God told me to tell them that, all those who had been fighting against the Pastor and the vision he had given there; must either stop or be removed. I left that revival and came the next year to preach at the same church. I discovered in that years time; 12 people from that ministry had died. It was a very somber discovery to say the least. Yet, I realized the God we serve, in this day and hour will not suffer his purpose to be hindered any longer. Well-meaning saints who believe with all their heart that they are doing the will of God, will go on into eternity, because of their unwillingness to hear the word **(vision)** of the Lord and come submissive to his purpose. So then, God will raise up those who will be absolutely obedient. This is the ushering in of the final anointing; and this move of the Spirit of God, shall reveal the very presence and power of God in the Church as a body ministry. There will never again be the 12 in one Pastor. **(All things to all people)** But the weight of the ministry in the Church will be a true unveiling of every part of the body in its place and functioning according to it's measure in Grace. It is and will be an awesome manifestation of the Word of God in ***"The One New Man."*** Ephesians 2:15; gives us a picture of that which is taking place in the Spirit; *"Having abolished in His flesh the enmity; even the law of commandments contained in ordinances; for to make in himself of twain one New*

11

Man, so making peace." It is exciting to note here, that the Church has been called to walk in one heart, whether Jew or Greek. God has removed the barriers of separation and yet the Church has allowed the enemy **(the devil)** to steal its wholesomeness and vitality. It has only walked in a partial anointing because of its incorporation of the purposes of men, operating in the will of the flesh; and not the Spirit of God. This has been the motivation and direction of Satan against the body of Christ. It is to prevent Gods purpose from coming to fullness in Christ's body; the Church.

We can see the parallel to the Old Testament believers and understand the intent of Satan's opposition to the body of Christ. Yet, know this beloved, that the Church is on the verge of the greatest triumph and victory to ever be witnessed by men to the things of God. It is such a joy and blessing to be a part of the wondrous and supernatural work of the Spirit in this day and hour. This hour will usher in the fullness of Christ into the World through the Church walking in total and complete obedience to Him. The Church will be the image and likeness of God and is called and chosen to serve. Ephesians 4:24; tells us, *"that ye put on the new man which after God is created in righteousness and true holiness."* This is a blessed day and hour for the body of Christ indeed.

Chapter Two

"Must Needs"
vs. 4:4

Lets understand the significance of the hour we live in. It is such a time to know the urgency of the Spirit, and move with directness and boldness. For the whole will of God; **(his purpose)** is the destiny of the Church. Jesus when he knew that the Pharisees had heard how he baptized more believers then John; Jn. 4:1; He left Judea, and departed again to Galilee. Vs. 3 This is an important statement in the scripture because our walk in Christ is not dependant upon what other men think. Christ knew that they would ridicule and scorn him even as they had already hardened themselves to his ministry. Much of the time there is a resistance to the desire of God in our hearts, because it is unacceptable to men. Often, there is a acceptance to the tradition rather than obedience to observe the commandments of God. When Christ begins to speak to the heart of an individual; it is more important to obey his directives, then to follow after the dictates of men. Jesus in Mark 7:7 taught saying; *"How be it in vain they worship me, teaching for doctrines the commandments of Men." In verse 13, he tells them; Making the Word of God of none effect, through your traditions which ye have delivered, and many such like things do ye."* Let us define this term commandment. Webster shows: It is a order, or command: a command is the ability to control, or activate a device by means of a signal, or a body of troops under a commander and area or position that one commands, a position of highest authority So then, this is a hard word that is come from the Lord in regard to the intent and purpose of the Father: That we as good soldiers must show ourselves obedient to Christ as our commander and chief. The Apostle Paul tells son Timothy; *"fight the good fight of faith, lay hold on eternal life, whereunto thou art also called, and hast professed a good profession before many witnesses".* 1 Tim. 6:12 Our task as the people of the Lord Jesus

Christ, is one of extreme significance to His purpose and will. Our place in Him and the keeping of his word will affect those that are around us and draw them into the kingdom of God. Christ is in us redeeming man to himself. Even as those of that generation were responsible for the prophetic anointing of that day; so are those of this day responsible for Gods prophetic word and purpose in the earth today. Not that men can do the will of God apart from God, but that with obedience and submission; God through men can do his pleasure. We must do and say what He himself does and says! We must allow God to command us and direct us. We are His troops and His device in the earth to fulfill his purpose. Christ is the Commander In Chief. Now, no one who is a soldier operates independently of the command structure.

In John 4:4, we see a compelling in Christ which draws him out of one city and into another. **He must needs go to Samaria.** When we know the purpose in our lives for what God has intended; we can move directly and with assertiveness. There is then, a zeal and determination in our hearts to fulfill his charge. We are a Spirit led organism: first individually, then collectively as the body of Christ. The Lord is driven by the leading of the Spirit, to go to this city because of the specific purpose of the Father to be revealed there. Sometimes, we miss the will of the Lord; in that we don't recognize his leading. We are come into the hour where Gods people will be yet more sensitive to the leading of the Spirit of God. Many souls and lives are dependant on the message of the Gospel of Jesus Christ in us. We are the ones chosen to fulfill the call of God in this end time. We are not chosen because of our brilliance or astuteness; not even for our elegance and grace. We are chosen for our willingness to obey Christ. God simply wants a yielded vessel. In this day of much confusion in the lives of men and women concerning their purpose for being here; there has been a steady quest for peace and a state of mind that satisfies the emptiness in many hearts. The use of such things, like drugs whether prescription or illegal, are a major witness for how many people are seeking to satisfy a long missing need in their lives. What is it that is missing in them? What is it that is causing them to search out ways to satisfy that longing? The answers to these questions are understood first in the need of every man to worship. They are secondly, seen in the need to understand one's purpose for existing and discovering the mind of Christ for our lives and how to accomplish his commanded will for us. In the book of Ecclesiastes 12:13; *"Let us hear the conclusion of the whole matter: fear God and keep his commandments."* **(Orders)** The provision of the immutable God through the shedding of the matchless blood of Jesus gives men asylum from the fears of living without purpose or meaning in life. There can be no substitute for relationship with the living God. Men have made millions of dollars and still walked in empty shells unfulfilled and without wholeness of being; because they did not have relationship with the one who gives meaning and purpose to what they accomplished: *("inasmuch as, he who buildeth the house is greater than the house.")* Heb. 3:3b. There is no life without Christ that is meaningful; *He who hath the Son hath life, and he who hath not the Son of God, hath not life."* I Jn. 5:12

Now, lets view this from where men are who live apart from relationship with Christ. Is there any wonder why there is great pressure placed on the medical community to produce drugs which will cure the ills of entire nations. This is the spiritual placebo for what men desire to receive without obedience to Christ. The medical profession however, lacks the skill to produce that which is spiritual in nature and discerned through Gods Holy Spirit; and completely opposed to the flesh. This is not an indictment against the medical profession, but a sobering statement of truth. We understand that the medical profession is a usable and serviceable gift to men in this world system and even the wisdom and knowledge come from God. However, they cannot bridge the gap in spiritual things. Romans 8:5 declares; *that* *"For they that are after the flesh do mind the things of the flesh; but they that are after the Spirit, the things of the Spirit. vs. 6 For to be carnally minded is death; but to be spiritually minded is life and peace."* Albeit, the medical profession is just one avenue that men use to try to discover wholeness, yet, it is not the only way that men use. It is projected in sexual fantasy magazines, physical fitness themes, video games, survival ritual games and other escapes. We cannot begin to persuade men, of the fallacy of many efforts. These are displays of the heart to prove by skill and ability their sense of worth. The world system cannot cure the ills of a people which are spiritually deficient and sin sick.   Romans. 3:24; gives us the license and remedy for these ills. *"Being justified freely by his grace through the redemption that is in Christ Jesus vs.25 Whom God hath set forth to be a propitiation through faith in his blood to declare righteousness for the remission of sins that are past through the forbearance of God."* It is a just God that has given his Son to satisfy his righteous demands for sin, He, (Jesus Christ) is the only remedy. Even as, Christ was compelled to go to Samaria a city of Sychar, (vs.5): the Lord is stopping in every place in this day and hour to accomplish his purpose in a people who will receive Him. It is the joy of Christ to come and dwell in us.

Now, when the Lord comes to us; he always has a specific reason and purpose in mind. God never does anything without purpose. His focus in us always concerns not only His will in us; but His will for those with whom we interact. It is the will of God that pleases Him. When the Lord speaks of His will concerning the Lord Jesus Christ and what he must suffer for the sins of man kind: He commands Isaiah to write; *"Yet it pleased the Lord to bruise Him; he hath put him to grief; when thou shalt make his soul and offering for sin, he shall see his seed, he shall prolong his days, and the pleasure of the Lord shall prosper in His hand."* Isa. 53:10   The character of the Lord is revealed in His desire to fulfill in Christ the purpose of God the Father. This is the very heart of what the Lord is looking for in true believers. Not just a willingness to receive the blessings of God; but acceptance of the whole purpose of the Father, regardless of the cost or price. What we are willing to endure for the sake of Christ is the first step toward satisfying his purposes in us. Jesus then, in coming into Samaria, knew that he must be at the place he was led to of the Spirit; to accomplish the mission he was given.. NOTE: The term Led of the Spirit, is for our realization. Christ as the example in the flesh for us demonstrates to the church, the necessity of following after the Spirit of God. Yet, he is the fullness of God. *"For it pleased the Father, that in Him should all fullness dwell."* Col.1:19 Everything that is to be accomplished in us by the Father; has an established pattern in Jesus Christ. Now the Lord has a task for us that is yet the mission of the Son: to destroy the old traditions and patterns which men reverence.

Jacob's well is the place where he is to come. He sees a woman he knows would come to this place at this hour. **(Sixth).** Jesus confronts the woman by asking for a drink of water. Jn 4:7   This Samaritan Woman wants to know why Jesus being a Jew, would ask her, a Samaritan, for something to drink. (Vs.8) *"for the Jews have no dealings with the Samaritans."* Again, there is prejudice in the Church today: many types of spiritual segregation, which separate Gods people. Not merely racial or color issues which many think to be the only one and most significant separation, but there are doctrinal issues and barriers regarding the role of women in spiritual things. This is not the desire of Christ. It is a sin condition, which has devastated the body of believers; in that we have not the power to fight an effective warfare against the enemy of our soul; because of our lack of love one for another.

Some would wonder how this is become an issue of love. As a Pastor in the body of Christ; it is my job to teach people how to love one another. This in itself is a great task, yet, it is not just the responsibility for the inward workings of the local assembly, but the outward as well. It is the need of the ministry, for the Spirit of Christ in me to be imbibed into the spirits of those whom God has placed into my care. Now, if I possess not the right heart and spirit regarding the things of Christ; how can I effectively show and lead his people? This then means that they who lead are culpable for the heart of God and it's affect on God's people. It starts with his leaders first and foremost. Secondly, we must be confident that everything that God said is absolutely true and will stand. I do not need to argue or convince men of it's power and anointing, because the Word of God will defend and preserve it. The main question is will we believe Him. Thirdly; the Word will transform us into **SUCH**: his attributes become alive in us and we become the mirror image of Him. Heb. 1:3; *"who being the brightness of His glory, and the express image of His person, when He had by Himself purged our sins,* **(our segregations are sin)**_*sat down at the right hand of the Majesty on high;"* the Word of God will bring us into the love of God and that grace which is able to transform us into his image. This is the inward responsibility of the ministry. Yet, in the outward aspect of this; we find that if leadership does not do the effective task of pouring into it's membership, there will be a

17

great resistance to corporate relationship. This is the coming together of the body of Christ in unity and love. Spiritual division is only a part of the yoke to be broken and the change which is to come. The Holy Spirit is working in the body of Christ to break every yoke. The blood and power of the risen savior has prevailed and cannot be diffused through the will of men. Neither will Christ allow the effectiveness of purpose to be deterred for the sake of men.

It takes a body that is healthy and whole; nurtured in the truth of Gods word and empowered by the Holy Ghost, to defeat Satan. Sin leaves the body crippled and maimed and unable to combat the adversary because of our weakened condition. The Apostle Paul told the Church at Corinth; *"Now I beseech you brethren, by the name of our Lord Jesus Christ, that ye shall all speak the same thing, and that there be no divisions among you; but that you are perfectly joined together in the same mind and the same judgement."* Cor. 1:10. The Church has lacked in its unity and agreement together. It has suffered because of its lack of love and its separation. There should be no divisions among them which name the name of Christ. Love is the very heart and essence of Gods character. It is limitless and without boundaries. We could never recover through sacrifice what we lose in being disobedient.

Now God is calling for a new place of love and respect in the body. We cannot be conditional as the people of God, in our love for one another. It is unacceptable to Christ. Jesus shows the Samaritan women that there is indeed a difference in Him and what she knew to be true in Judaism. There is a difference between us and the rest of the world. We offer the love and righteousness of the living God. We are His representatives and his disciples for Christ's sake. Jesus informed this woman, that if she had recognized the gift of God; she would have ask of Him; And he would have given her living water. Vs.10. We have the waters of life, to offer to every man. It is the purpose of every servant to please his Master, and the people of God are His servants to fulfill His desire in the earth. We must offer the righteous Christ to everyone. It is he that will satisfy the hearts and longings of men. Jesus told his disciples;

"And I, if I, be lifted up from the earth, will draw all men unto me." Jn. 12:32 The people of the Lord must lift up the Lord Jesus; that men will be saved and set free. Jesus came to offer this Samaritan woman, eternal life. He had come to free her from the hunger of her soul. She did not understand as yet, that what He offered her was a new life; but she asked questions of him to satisfy her curiosity. How would he get this water since that well was so deep? How would he get this water without something to draw it with? Are you greater than our Father Jacob? Vs.11-12. Christ was not nervous because of her questions. He answered her in the wisdom of the Spirit. The people of God must be ready to accept the challenges of the world. We offer the Living Christ; yet they have many questions in their lives which must be answered. We do not answer in our wisdom, but the wisdom of Jesus Christ. The Word of God declares; "But of him are ye in Christ Jesus, who of God is made unto us wisdom, and righteousness, and sanctification, and redemption." 1 Cor.1:30 Christ is made all things to us that we might fulfill the will of God. Furthermore, it is shown by the scripture in verse 31, "that according as it is written. He that glorieth, let Him glory in the Lord." Christ's accomplishment in the Church is not because of the strength and abilities of the believer; but of the Living God in us. God will not allow us to take His glory as our own. It has been shameful, the pride and arrogance of men in the religious world, who have tried to usurp the glory of the living God. God will give glory to his people in the culmination and fulfillment of his plan. But, it then becomes a gift and not a theft. John writes in John 17:22; "And the glory which thou gavest me I have given them; that they may be one, even as we are one."

The Father will reveal His glory in His sons; for we have been chosen to do his whole desire from the foundations of the world. We are chosen to bring the world the manifestation of the purposes of God. Jesus said in Jn. 17:3; "and this is life eternal, that they may know thee the only true God, and Jesus Christ whom thou has sent." **We must needs go through Samaria.** There is a work that the Body of Christ must perform in this day and hour to fulfill the purpose of Christ. It is not optional, in terms of Gods sovereign plan, for the believer. We do however, have the right not to serve or do that which has been given to us to accomplish. We are moral agents and can option to not do as the Lord has desired, but with dire consequences. Dire in that, God will not force us to serve Him, nor will he promote our foolishness. It is the heart and desire of the Lord that we will serve him willingly and with all our heart; but he cannot allow his plan and purpose to go unaccomplished. The Church has sought the heart of the Lord on occasion, but in coming to this time and hour; it has been inconsistent in its motivation for the fullness of the will and heart of God. It has occupied the same venue as the Churches in Revelation.

In the church of Pergamos they held the doctrine of Balaam. The teaching of Balaam, was a doctrine which cast a stumbling block before the people of the Lord. *Rev. 2:14*   Also, there is a church at Ephesus which John the Revelator says; *"Nevertheless, I have somewhat against thee, because thou has left thy first Love."* Rev. 2:4   There is a move of the Spirit of the Lord, to reconcile men back to God and remove the teaching of Balaam. **(Doctrine of intermarriage with the heathen nation)** For the Church of today, it is the willingness to accept such things as the new age philosophies. These are Eastern cultic beliefs and other damnable heresies and teachings, that call for the merging of mystic wisdom with the truth of the Holy God of Creation. When men add to the truth, it is error, and when they take away from the truth, it is error. The Church of this generation will be a people of great understanding in the Word of God. It will not be subject to the lies of that Wicked. John declares in the book 1 John 2:20, *"but ye have an unction from the Holy One and ye know all things."* The World will be exposed to the truth of God in the Church. It is a word and wisdom of the Lord Jesus that will be irrefutable. Not only will it be irrefutable, but it will be born out with great demonstration. *"These signs shall follow them that believe; in my name shall they cast out devils; they shall speak with new tongues Mk 16:17;; vs. 18. They shall take up serpents; and if they drink any deadly thing, it shall not hurt them; they shall lay hands on the sick, and they shall recover."* God will make visible his presence and power in the Church even as there was a visible difference in Christ for all the world to see.

CHAPTER THREE

JACOB' WELL
vs. 6

Now, let us digress briefly to an area of our lives which many have trouble in. Jesus in coming into Samaria, (**Sychar**): comes into contact with a woman of Samaria at Jacob's well. Jacob's well is the place of great significance to the well being of that city. He came at the sixth hour, which is noontime. Many at that time, would be preparing to gather water in their vessels. The parallel we must see, are the lives of many; that are lost to the purposes of Christ. This passage of the word of God, gives us a view of Christ's concern for being in the place where God the Father has appointed him to meet with this lost woman, and give to her the water of life. This well represents life to the people of that community, but Jesus brings the promise of living waters and that they would not thirst again.

Often, it is difficult to change the things that people put their confidence in. It is equally as difficult to get men to see that there is something greater than Jacob's well. Sometimes, we can't let go, because of the need to feel secure in what we have; or to be comfortable with familiar surroundings. Many depend on their condition (**where they live, or what they possess, or who they know etc.**) to be the source of their grounding in life. Much of the time, because of these conditions and the perspectives men create; there is a warfare that prevails. It is a warfare that prevails against them and those who will bring the message of Christ in this struggle. Satan does not want us to let go of the things which have separated us from the purpose of the Lord. We have a hardship because of flesh; or because of a lack of knowledge. That is why; when we discover the truth of God; we must mix it with faith. Hebrews 4:2 says concerning Israel *"The Word preached did not profit them not being mixed with faith in them that heard it."* Revelation is the key to our overcoming those things in our lives that we struggle with. It allows us to take the anointing of truth and apply to our condition, which then becomes the rule for our living. It is the anointing that destroys the yoke. **(Isaiah 10:27)** This woman needed the Word of God. Note however; to be identified with Christ is to precipitate warfare and many will not give themselves to the battle. It is a question of faith and obedience to His commanded will.

Let us note that Jesus held two reasons for coming to that particular place. First, he knew that he was wearied and needed rest from his journey. We see in this the natural need of Christ: that he was wearied. John 4:6 Yet, the fact that he was tired did not keep him from being obedient to the purpose of the Father. As believers, we must understand that, there is a natural weariness to the flesh. However, it does not preclude what we are to do in the keeping of the desired purpose of the Father. Secondly, he knew this was the place he would find the Samaritan woman. She had become the focus of his mission there, and would be the catalyst for drawing many to the presence of the Lord. Often, the Lord will do the foolish things to confound the wise. He did not give the task to the Scribes and Pharisees. He taught these things to the weak and the rejected. The vision and purpose of the Lord is available to them that seek the kingdom of God first. While the Samaritan woman did not necessarily expect to find the Messiah at the well; she did not reject him because of the hunger in her heart. That hunger in her was for a lasting and satisfying relationship. She had had six husbands, but was unfulfilled and without purpose and direction in her life. There was a cry in her spirit that could be identified only by God. The Lord also tells us that, he would answer us and show us great and mighty things which we knew not; if we would but call on Him. Jer 33:3

The things of God are made visible to us when we desire the heart and mind of God. We must have a desire to fulfill His perfect will in our lives. The Lord further states in Heb. 6:1; "*Therefore leaving the principles of the doctrine of Christ, let us go unto perfection: not laying again the foundation of repentance from dead works and of faith toward God".* We must do that which is greater than the initial works of faith. We must go on unto perfection in Christ Jesus. Our only hope rests in Christ. Yet, this isn't a standard of not failing or of never making a mistake. It is the maturing of the people of the Lord into a dynamic and powerful church. This will be a vibrant and exciting body of believers which will walk in balance and order.

The Samaritan woman knew that her life lacked fulfillment. She also knew the needs of her community and what it lacked as well. Her first concern when given the revelation of life eternal was to go and tell everyone in the community to **"come see a man."** This then proves she was not comfortable with what she had, and now someone and something better was come: Jesus Christ. We have something better to look forward to; Christ has given us of himself. We can no longer afford to remain in the same circumstances, with the same attitudes and cares that have always impeded the process of the Spirit of Life in us. We are a *"peculiar people, a people of his own* "to *show forth the praises of Him that hath called us out of darkness into marvelous light."* 1 Pe. 2:9 This Samaritan woman was being challenged by the living Christ to come into faith and believe on him as Lord and Savior; there should be a confidence that we possess, because of the redemptive quality of the gift in us. We cannot allow that the blessing of the Lord shall pass us by, because we have a comfort zone that we operate in. There is necessity laid upon us to seek the mind of God and receive the direction of His spirit in our walk.

Jacob's well is what was given to sustain them in the past. It is no longer the method, or the wisdom, that God chooses to use in this day and hour. Isaiah reports; *"Remember ye not the former things, neither consider the things of old. Behold I will do a new thing; now it shall spring forth; shall ye not know it? I will even make a way in the wilderness, and rivers in the desert."* Isa. 43:18-19 There has come the One, to this Samaritan woman; who is able to transform her life, and the life of that community. She was the one chosen for **Such a time as then,** to witness the awesome gift and blessing of the Lord. She had not realized the gift of God: eternal life through faith in the Son of God. Many in this hour that we live in have not recognized the gift of God. The witness of the Son is given to them, and there is a resistance and hardness; which blinds the hearts of men to the truth. For this reason, the Church must pray as never before, that God will make hearts more tender to the truth of Christ. This woman, now having come into discourse with the Son; becomes quite curious about what he purposes to give her. **(living water).** She desires to know whether he is greater than her Father Jacob. Many desire, even in this present time to know whether or not, what we offer them is greater than what has been given them already. Is Christ the answer to the troubles of my family? Can he bring joy and victory to every area of my life? In raising these issues; John 4:12, *"Art thou greater than our Father Jacob, which gave us the well, and drank thereof himself, and his children, and his cattle?"* Jesus replies here with the wisdom of the Spirit; *vs. 13* by comparing the natural water with the Word. *"Whosoever, drinketh of this water shall thirst again."* He then assures her that; *"Whosoever drinketh of the water that I shall give him shall never thirst; but, the water that I shall give him, shall be in him a well of water springing up into everlasting life."* We have this assurance as believers; that Jesus Christ is the all-sufficient one, and he is the provider for all. The Apostle Paul in his admonishment of the Ephesians; tells them that his prayer for them is; *"That Christ may dwell in your hearts by faith; that ye, being rooted and grounded in Love, may be able to comprehend with all saints what is the breath, and length, and depth, and height; and to know the Love of Christ, which passeth knowledge, that ye might be filled with all the fullness of God."*

The message of our Savior to us in this hour has not changed. There is a reality to serving the living God. The believer must come into an active and aggressive relationship of faith, in Jesus Christ. Now, there can be no hesitation on the part of God's people to seek Him in faith; *(" the just shall live by faith")*. Rom. 1:17 In the quest of the believer to know the righteousness of the God of our salvation; we are assured that God will reveal the mysteries of Christ in us. Paul goes further to say; *"Now unto him that is able to do exceeding abundantly above all that we can ask or think, according to the power that worketh in us."* Eph. 3:20   In this, it is revealed to the

Ephesians that there is power that works in the believer. This is the power which performs in us; the exceeding abundantly of Christ; and it will work above and beyond all that we can ask or think. It is His power. In this, we find that there is no limit to be placed on Him who called us. What then limits the greatness of God; who created all things in the universe?

Often we desire to know how His Will will be performed in us. There is a worry or a fear, even constraints; because we cannot fathom the depth of the grace of Christ manifest to us. This is a relationship of trust. It is not based on any pre-conceived notion or whim. It is the vastness of the living Christ that is given to us. Whosoever will drink in these waters of life; shall not despair over the ability of the risen King to keep them. But you must drink first, and then continue to drink of His righteousness and peace. The woman then asks in vs.15; *"Sir give me this water, that I thirst not, neither come hither to draw."* She had become eager to receive this water. There is however, an immediate need in her life that is pointed out by the Lord. In vs. 16, he tells her to *"Go call thy husband, and come hither."* She admits to the Lord, that she does not have a husband in vs. 17. Jesus then points out the serious problem that exists in her life: Sin. *"For thou hath had five husbands; he whom thou now hath is not thy husband: in that saidst thou truly."* vs. 18. Here, the woman has admitted to Jesus that she has no husband: Jesus receives her confession and proceeded to point out that she is yet in sin.

At this point men must realize that the sovereign God has seen the sins of all men. He knows where we stand in him. The woman did not try to conceal her sin, but, she spoke the truth. You must yield yourself to righteousness in all things. The true believer is not one who assents to the Word of God in his mind. They are the believers, who believe and obey through the Spirit. She, having been confronted with her sin; began to perceive that Christ was a prophet. Immediately, her focus turns to worship. The question that faces every person on a daily and individual basis is one of worship. Whatever and whomever is your idol; you will worship. Therefore, in confessing and repenting of our sins, we are free to

25

worship the true and living God. When we have a greater readiness to confess our sins and repent: we will have a greater ability to worship. This is the first most critical step in entering into the presence of the Lord. The second step is to obey his word. The evidence of our love for Him is our obedience to Him. As we carry out the commands of scripture, we can see the pattern for our entry into His holy presence: Psalm 100:1-4 declares; *"Make a joyful noise unto the Lord, all ye lands. Serve the Lord with gladness; come before his presence with singing.* Note: it is a spiritual impossibility to come into the presence of the Lord in our songs of praise, when known sin is unconfessed or unrepented of. Our praise is the heart of our relationship with the Lord and should be predicated on a heart-felt relationship of obedience. The evidence of our obedience to Christ is our submission to his Word. *(The people of the Lord must see that our call is an active commitment, to the incarnate Word Himself.)* To enter his presence, is to come by relationship to that Word. *"Know ye that the Lord, he is God; that it is he who hath made us, and not we ourselves; we are his people and the sheep of his pasture. Enter into his gates with thanksgiving, and into his courts with praise; be thankful unto him, and bless his name."* This is the strength of our fellowship and union with Christ. We enter into the presence of the Father, through the veil of Christ which was rent in twain. Who then, can enter in, but those who walk in relationship with Him. ***"He ever liveth, to make intercession for us."*** How can we deny the depth of His truth to perform in us the mandate of God's revelation which is given to the believer. Therefore, having believed on Him, we walk even as Christ himself walked.

In walking out the revelation that He has given; we give Him praise and glory for having brought change to our hearts and mind. The Apostle Paul speaks regarding the boundless blessing that causes through us thanksgiving to God. He further admonishes that by the administration of the Holy Spirit there is a supply for the wants of the saints but is made more abundant by many thanksgivings unto God. Praise brings the presence of God. When his presence has come we begin to worship Him. As we then worship Him; God reveals our frailty and shortcomings. This is not to wound or hurt us although it may at times be hard to take. It is to allow us to become conformed to his image and likeness. Bless the name of the Lord God forever!!

Now, everything Satan desired to do in and against the believer; revolves around worship. There was sin in the heart of Satan that caused his downfall. There was a desire to be worshiped in the stead of the creator; God. Isaiah 14:12-14, gives us the picture of what took place in heaven against God. *"How art thou fallen from heaven, Oh Lucifer, Son of the morning! How art thou cut down to the ground, which did weaken the nations! For thou hath said in thy heart, I will ascend into heaven, I will exalt my throne above the stars of God: I will sit also upon the mount of the congregation, in the sides of the North: I will ascend above the heights of the clouds; I will be like the Most High."* Everything that we do in this life is a question of worship. For the Samaritan woman, to serve and worship Christ, she must realize that sin is against the character of God. She then must give up the will of her flesh to receive the redemptive work of Christ. Again the Apostle Paul phrases it in these terms: *"Therefore if any man be in Christ, he is a new creature: the former things are passed away; behold all things are become new."* 2 Cor. 5:17 There is a certain reality to newness of life in the Spirit of Christ: several points are evident.

Firstly, that all men will be accountable for the life of Christ slain at Calvary. Whether we have received Christ or not; there will be an accountability made for his blood. This accountability will be given regardless of men's willingness to submit to the plan of God for their lives. *(every knee shall bow and every tongue confess)* It will not prevent the Word of God from bringing the judgment of God to every heart. The second is one of confession and repentance of sin; with no regard for the thoughts and opinions of men. The Samaritan Women is concerned about Jacob's well being the place of inheritance. She talks of the greatness of her father Jacob. Jacob's well is not the place of our inheritance. Jesus assures her that whosoever drinketh of this water shall thirst again; but the water which he shall give, shall be in him a well of water springing up into eternal life. Jn. 4:13-14 We have our inheritance in Christ Jesus. *"That in the dispensation of the fullness of times he might gather together in one all things in Christ, both which are in heaven, and which are on earth; even in Him: in whom also we have obtained an inheritance, being predestined according to purpose of Him who worked all things together after the counsel of His will.*" Eph. 1:10-11   So then, we are persuaded to hold on to the things of our Father. We then receive the fullness of life in Jesus Christ.

Thirdly; the traditions of men and the rudiments wherein they are established will be cast down by the wisdom of the living Christ. We will see in this day and hour; a powerful move of God, to bring men and women into an exciting and mighty move of the Spirit. The works of evil will be destroyed by the anointing of the Holy Ghost. God is going to use the trodden and the cast out: **(cast out of the hierarchy of religion);** to win many souls unto the Lord Jesus Christ in this hour. God is going to use the un-churched to be instrumental in the completing of His purposes, in this end time ministry. Those whom men have discarded and given up on as lost, are the ones Christ will draw by his Spirit to accomplish his pleasure in the earth. " *Where is the wise? Where is the scribe? Where is the disputer of the world? Hath not God made foolish the wisdom of this world? For after that in the wisdom of God, the world by wisdom knew not God, it pleased God by the foolishness of preaching to save them that believe.*" 1 Cor. 1:20-21. When men had the ability and knowledge to do the will of God, they did not do it. God has chosen to use them that would, in the foolishness of preaching; be obedient to the will of God. We will begin to see the evidence of this in the Word of God; later in the book.

CHAPTER FOUR

THE PLACE OF WORSHIP
vs. 20

Beloved, in the face of the blessings of God, in Christ Jesus; there will be a turning away from the power of God. The Word reveals to us; *"That in the last days perilous times shall come. For men shall be lovers of their own selves, covetous, boasters, proud, blasphemers, disobedient to parents, unthankful, unholy, without natural affection, truce breakers, false accusers, incontinent, fierce, despisers of those that are good; traitors, heady, high minded, lovers of pleasures more than lovers of God; having a form of godliness, but denying the power thereof; from such turn away."* The Word of God in its fullness will not be received by every one. Men who have their own agendas will continue to walk in the imagination of their own hearts. They will not according to the Word of God endure sound doctrine. Many will depart from the faith, giving heed to seducing spirits and doctrines of devils. **(1Tim. 4:1)** There will be lies in hypocrisy; of men whose consciences have been seared with a hot iron. Vs.2 This means that they have been cut off from the truth and conviction of the Spirit of God; which reproves men of their sins. Without the conviction of the Spirit of God; acting upon our conscience; we cannot have a repentant heart or even the desire to seek forgiveness. Without the spirit of repentance working in us, or the desire to seek the forgiveness of the Lord Jesus for our sins; we cannot worship God. Jesus told the Samaritan woman, that she worshiped she knew not what. **(Jn.4:22)** She believed that the place of worship, was the place her Father's worshiped. She argues with him that they say, **The Jews)**, that Jerusalem is the place men ought to worship. Vs. 21 Jesus replies to her that, *"the Jews know what they worship: For salvation is of the Jews."* Paul then declares in his letter to the Romans. *"What advantage than, hath the Jew? Rom. 3:1a; Much every way; chiefly, because unto them were committed the oracles of God."* vs. 2 There is a clarity here, of the plan of God, which is manifest in all of its parts. It is made known in the Jews, and to the Greeks. The Apostle Paul develops this knowledge of the truth, by pointing out, that we as Gentile believers are grafted into a good olive tree. **(Israel being the good olive tree)** See: Rom.11:24 God furthermore, will not be denied the fullness of consummation: we become the Church of God in Christ Jesus. We are not a denomination but we are the Bride of Christ and have been betrothed by God.

We find then in this; that, worship is not the place per se, where we come to. It is not the mountain or the city we reside in. We do not worship because of the people; though we can worship with other people. Worship is not the perfection of stuff and things around us; God is not concerned with the external but the internal. He is not concerned with the outward appearance but the heart. Jesus told the religious order of that day; *"Woe unto you Scribes and Pharisees, hypocrites! For ye are like whited sepulchers, which indeed appear beautiful outward, but are within full of dead men's bones, and of all uncleaness."* Mt. 23:27   It is not the time in which we do it; but it can take time, nor is it the music that is made; although music can help usher in the presence of God. It is not our eloquence of speech; nor is God intimidated by the words we use, or who is leading in the devotion: Although, the devotion leader should desire His heart. Worship is the personal relationship that we have with the sovereign God. It is the expression of our hearts for who He is, and what Jesus has done. Jesus said; *"The hour cometh, and now is, when the true worshipers shall worship the Father in Spirit and truth: for the **Father seeketh such** to worship Him." God is a spirit and they that worship him must worship him in spirit and in truth."* Jn. 4:23-24   Herein is the wisdom. God revealed to us in this day and hour that worship of the living God is according to who he is. It is not because of our righteousness, or our abilities and gifting. God is looking for a specific relationship with himself; and an attitude in the believer, because of that relationship with Him. We have seen many substitutes in the religious world for worship and for relationship with God. Yet, it is discovered in the Word; that these things that men call Holy unto the Lord; are far from being holy and acceptable with Him; whereby the Lord is not pleased. In many instances, they are strange fire and hypocrisy to Him. God showed the children of Israel, that he would not accept the sacrifice and worship of the sons of Aaron; when they presented themselves improperly. They offered incense to the Lord; the symbol of worship as offered before the Lord, in the old covenant. It was in will worship, that they rendered unto the Lord.

The Word points out the flaw of *"men being beguiled of their reward in a voluntary humility and worshiping of angels, intruding into those things which he hath not seen,* ___(they had not seen Him in His glory)___ *vainly puffed up by a fleshly mind, and not holding the Head from whom all the body by joints and bands having nourishment ministered, and knit together, increaseth with the increase of God."* Col. 2:18-19 God not only wants to receive our worship but to impart into the character of his people that we may reflect Him. When they offered the incense; *(worship)* it was strange unto the Lord God. God then consumed them with fire from His presence. Lev. 10:2   Moses began to reveal to Aaron, This is it that the Lord spoke saying: *"I will be sanctified in them that come nigh me, and before all the people I will be glorified.* Vs. 3 Now, the desire of the Lord is one of receiving pure worship from a people: whose hearts and minds are consumed in Him.

The incense of our worship; is magnified in the offering of ourselves before Him as a living sacrifice unto God. Rom. 12:1   There is a consuming in Him, that transforms us into His image through the relationship we enjoy in His Son. We do not come in the strength of our will; but in the blood of His anointing. We must offer to the Lord His righteousness: not the forced worship of our will and flesh. There is a parallel to this forced worship found in Daniel the third chapter. It is the commanded worship of men based upon the sound of certain instruments and all kinds of music. It was the forced worship of a Golden image that was set up by King Nebuchadnezzar. Dan.3:5   We find there to be an intolerance for the worship of men in the spirit. This was part of the difficulty which Jesus faced with the religious Fathers of that day. They had become accustomed to patterns of worship; and regulations in worship. Anyone who would do contrary to the established norms, were rejected. Jesus having healed a man who was blind from birth; showed the blindness of the leadership of that day. It was pointed out in John Chapter 9, Vs. 41: Jesus said unto them, *"If ye were blind, ye would have no sin; but now ye say, we see; therefore your sin remaineth."* They were so bogged down in their traditions and in the will of the flesh: they were unable to accept the work of the Spirit of God. We cannot become so bound in our will and steeped in our traditions that we fail to allow the move of the Holy Spirit in our lives and ministries. If we allow the traditions which have separated us from the will and presence of God, to continue to manifest because of our stubbornness and hardness of heart: there will be a holding back of the power in our lives. This is the power of the Lord which is on the move in the Spirit.

There is a shaking in the Spirit which is coming to the Body of Christ. It is coming through the Spirit of Almighty God; to bring a full revival to the people of God. There is a mighty manifestation of the Sons of God; on the verge of exploding in the purposes and intent of Christ. We are being prepared by Him to fulfill all His desire. Therefore, when we worship; it must be born in us out of a pure desire for Christ, and to render ourselves to him. It is a yielding to God in adoration and exaltation of His greatness. It is not born of a desire to exalt ourselves and those with whom we fellowship; but it is purely unto Him who is the strength and joy of life. Christ reminds us that God is a spirit. There is only one way to approach Him: that is in the spirit. Any other attempt to approach Him is futile at best. *"That which is flesh is flesh and: They that are after the flesh, do mind the things of the flesh: but they that are after the spirit, do mind the things of the spirit."* Rom. 8:5 *"The one to whom you yield yourself to obey; his servant ye are.* Rom. 6:16 We must yield ourselves unto the true and Living Christ; to obey His commands. Jesus points out to us in Vs. 23 of John 4 ***"That the hour cometh and now is"*** You cannot afford to sit in the same old place spiritually, that you have occupied from the beginning of your life in Christ. God is expectant that we will grow and progress in our relationship with Him. It is a constant move in the Spirit of God. We rise up in the will of His spirit, to advance as an army to the war that rages in the earth today. This warfare is not that which we see in the street or on television broadcasts in other nations and places. These things are merely a manifestation of those things which are working in the realm of the spirit. This warfare is a move in the spirit realm by Satan to destroy the work of Christ in the earth. The trouble and conditions which exist in the world: exist because of a constant barrage of spirit warfare in the heavenlies. Our call as ministers of righteousness is to go out into the very heart of Satan ruled territories, which are strongholds for his diabolical purposes. God in Christ Jesus is raising up a warrior like people that will stand in the limitless authority of the great and mighty God. Satan will flee in the face of the mighty armies of the Holy King.!!!!!!!!

CHAPTER FIVE

GOD IS A SPIRIT
vs. 24

In previous chapters, we stated that; *"God is a Spirit: and them that worship Him, must worship Him in spirit and in truth."* Jn. 4:24 This is quite significant to the purposes of God. His people do seek after Him; not by the will of the flesh, but the will of the spirit. Many have refuted the existence of God, because they are unable to see Him, or touch Him. They have, as have most all of mankind thought; that by the natural senses, they could know and perceive Him. It is not possible to know the presence of the God of all creation merely through the natural man. Men have always known that God exists, and that He created all things in heaven and in earth. We can see that all creation declares His greatness. *"Even, The invisible things of Him, from the creation of the world are clearly seen, being understood by the things that are made, even His eternal power and Godhead; so that they are without excuse."* Rom. 1:20 There is no excuse for men not recognizing the great and mighty God. Israel had forgotten the greatness of the God they served, and had become steeped in carnality. They had turned to the pagan gods of their enemies and captors.

The parallel of this turning away from the relationship of truth and obedience; is compelling even in this day. It is the same spirit that is desirous of bringing the people of God into bondage, again. The Word of God shows us the problem for men not being able to have a communion with Him that pleases Him. Rom. 8:6 *"for to be carnally minded is death; but to be spiritually minded is life and peace."* There is a need to crucify the flesh, with its affections and lusts. In Galatians 5:24; there is an evidence of our relationship with the Christ of our salvation: *" And they that are Christ's have crucified the flesh with its afflictions and lusts."* We find our hearts and minds pulled into the strength of the Word, when we obey it. The Word is the living and exciting manifestation of the character of Christ. *"In the beginning was the word, and the Word was with God, and the Word was God. The same was in the beginning with God."* Jn.1:1-2   Everything that is known of Him is manifested in the Word which became flesh and dwelt among men. Christ is that manifestation of the word of God to us. Vs. 14 We see in this then, that we are born of Him by the will of God. (*"Which are born, not of blood, nor of the will of the flesh, nor of the will of man."*)

We now, must take note that we are a triune being: body, soul and spirit. It is the complexity of this make-up, which drives us to search out the mysteries of a unique relationship with Christ. The body is the housing or temple for the soul and spirit. It is unique in its design, and its ability to carry out the physical demands of living in this world. It is highly adaptable to its surroundings and well equipped to make necessary adjustments to things around it. The Body however, is driven and motivated by its own innate desires and qualities. It has no desire to serve God or to please Him. It's will is to satisfy its passions and lusts according to its own purposes. It is void of any spiritual understanding or virtue. Therefore, it cannot please God. The Spirit truly is willing, but the flesh is weak.

In the Word of God we find that the Body has only one desire: it is to discover itself. The flesh man is eager to fulfill its purpose and not those of the living Christ. For this reason, the believer must recognize the temptations of the flesh. They lust to envy against the spirit. The body desires to manipulate and rule the spirit within man. If it is left to its own devices; the flesh will cause the whole man to be destroyed with the wickedness of sin and evil desire. This is why God destroyed all mankind in the day of Noah. Man had become so corrupt in the will of his flesh; that every imagination of his heart was only evil continually. Gen. 6:5 We live in just such an hour, when the imaginations of men, become the will of their flesh; and are ruled by their evil desire. Man has become more wicked and corrupt with the desire to please his lusts. John the Revelator speaks of the types of fleshly desires which tempt men continually. *"for all that is in the world, the lust of the flesh, and the lust of the eyes, and the pride of life, is not of the*

Father, but is of the world. And the world passeth away, and the lust thereof; but he that doth the will of God abideth forever." 1 John 2:16-17 Many are consumed with what their flesh wants. It is catered to, in the media, by television, radio, movies, magazines and newspapers. They are set-up through commercials which show; how great and necessary a product is through sexually suggestive themes. Our children are bombarded daily with the themes of those who are degenerate with the desires of the world around them. We do not see the themes of God and worship with any regularity or consistency; other than when we seek to know them, through that part of the media that indulges purely Christian values. Our children are pressed through games (**video**) of violence and of horror. They can play these games before they ever discover that there is a true and living God. Before they come into a understanding of what it is to worship and pray; they have already made to themselves other gods. It is this very heightened idolatry, which compels a society into degenerate moral values. There has been a desensitizing of children and families, through cartoons and through programming corrupt with the thoughts and ideas of a Christless class. It is the values of a society that is based on humanism and not on the tenets of the bible any longer and that by design. By the design of a vicious adversary; who looks to destroy the souls of men.

God is a spirit and we are a spirit motivated and directed people. The fact that we were made to worship is evident in what we do. Men have often become enamored with philosophies, and theologies; and much of what is sought after is errant to the purposes and desires of Jesus Christ. The press for the riches of this world has become to many times, the focal point of their desire and experience in life. Yet, we find in the Word of God; that *the love of money* has made corrupt the way of man. 1 Tim. 6:10 explains it this way; *"for the Love of money is the root of all evil: which while some coveted after, they have erred from the faith, and pierced themselves through with may sorrows;* but for the believer, Paul the Apostle says; *"But thou, O man of God, flee these things; and follow after righteousness, godliness, faith, love patience, meekness."* This is the heart of serving a God, who is desirous to be first in the lives of all men.

Now money is necessary in the world we live in, and God is not against the Christian having money or wealth. God is against the idolatry that develops, because men put money before Him. They become servants to their desire for wealth; rather than a desire to please the Father first. The bible is replete with many examples of wealthy men of God. Job was such an one, who even in the face of all he possessed; did not charge God foolishly. He served the Lord with all his heart and God asked Satan; *"hath thou considered my servant Job, that there is none like him in all the earth, a perfect and upright man, one that feareth God, and escheweth evil? And still he holdeth fast his integrity."* Job 2:3 God bragged on Job, because he was not clouded in his worship or desire to please the Lord. He was not an idol worshipper, in as much as he had not allowed his family and great wealth to effect his relationship with the living God. We cannot allow anything to separate us from the Love of God.

Wherefore then, do we build the foundation for a relationship with Him? It is not the practical resolve of men, or their abilities (**nor their strength**) that empowers their lives in the righteousness of Christ. It is the truth of His Word, and obedience to that which he has commended in us by faith that we build upon. It is what God the Father has spoken to us regarding His Son. Christ is the foundation for our righteousness in God. He is the gift which satisfies the demands of a just God. *"For other foundation can no man lay than that which is laid. which is Christ Jesus."* 1Cor. 3:11 The Church is then built upon the truth of God in Christ Jesus. Jesus himself said: *"I am they way, the truth, the life: no man cometh unto the Father but by me."* *John 14:6* None can approach the Father except through the Son. The character that God desires in us is that of His Son. Jesus is the perfect example to us and in us, for what God is raising up in the Church. In the past; men have done as it pleased them in the religious realm. They have set their hearts to fulfill their own pleasures and it caused a great brokenness in the Body of Christ. We have seen a cry for help in the Churches, which has left many people hurting and with unfulfilled needs. They have not been taught the Word of God which is necessary to complete victory in Christ Jesus in their lives. Christ is the answer for every need and in every occasion. If the Church is to come into total victory, it will do so because of men (**Man, woman, boy or girls)**; preaching and teaching the whole truth of God by the Spirit of God. The truth will not be saddled, with the inconveniences of men's thinking or opinions. The truth of Gods Word is the strength of all that will be accomplished in this end time by the Church. Whatever the Lord has spoken concerning His people, will surely come to pass. There is a move of the Spirit of God, in revelation knowledge and understanding. It is a move that will break the barriers which have come into place because of the traditions of men. The thoughts of men's hearts, which have possessed a form of Godliness deny the power of God. The truth will prevail in every place as the mandate of the scripture is primary and central to God's purpose and intent. (**heaven and earth will pass away before one jot or one tittle of my word fail)** Of course it becomes more critical because this is the end time, and God will bring **judgment** to the House of God first. It will be first; the tearing down of the walls of separation; because of color and race; and because of the spirit of error. The working of deceptions and confusions in the Church world, have caused havoc among ministries.

There has been a great fall among leaders on both the local and national levels. Severe bondage's have developed in the assemblies of Gods people on many levels. It is however, the move of the Spirit that has begun to come forth in this hour; that will break strongholds of the devil. When the people of God begin to embrace the will of His spirit; God will then empower His servants in great demonstration. His word is now coming alive in a very new and real way. The Word will not be denied the accomplishment of the purposes of the Lord in every place. There is a working in the Spirit; by the counsel of His will which shall establish Gods desire in the hearts of His people, to bring the broken and the trodden into healing and deliverance. The Church is the strength of Christ in this earth and it will not be denied in the fulfilling of the truth of God. There is a tremendous shaking of the very foundation of the Church world: in that the Lord Jesus will bring the people of God to a time of intense scrutiny. The bible declares; *"That the time is come when judgment must begin at the house of*

God; *and if it first begins at us, what shall the end of them that obey not the Gospel of God be?"* 1Peter 4:17   The Church is the driving force in the purposes of God in Christ; that all things will be fulfilled for His will.

CHAPTER SIX

THE FATHERS SUCH
JOHN 4:23

In order to know the requirements of God: We must go to His Word. By this we are able to discover His will and commandments for our lives. It is the word of God that enables us to acquire an understanding, first of who He is, and secondly; of the character of God. It is very important to know and understand the character of the God we serve. As we have touched on this in early discussions in this book: it is now necessary to go in depth with this discussion. This is the only way to enlarge our borders; so to speak, with the needed understanding. This then, will allow us to gain wisdom and insight into His requirements for us. The character of God is paramount to what we shall become in Him. It is noted in Peter 1:3-4 that; *"according as His divine power hath given unto us all things that pertain unto life and godliness, through the knowledge of Him that hath called us to glory and virtue: Whereby are given unto us exceeding great and precious promises: that by these ye might be partakers of the divine nature, having escaped corruption that is in the world through lust."* Yet, even as the power is given to us; there is no proper use, without the understanding of His nature and character. Whenever men use the things of God improperly; it becomes abuse. We have often seen many abuses in the Body of Christ, by those who say they know and understand but we find that they are short of the commandment of the Lord. Success in the Lord Jesus is predicated upon what is established by Him as the way of life in Him. Jesus is the way to fulfilling every part of the plan of God. Jesus told the Samaritan woman, that (**The Father Seeketh Such** vs. 4:23). We have briefly touched upon the fact that He (*Father*); desires true worshipers. Because worship is in the spirit; this combined with the truth of God; are primary components of revelation to the Samaritan woman. Christ showed her that God was looking for a specific type of relationship with the Father. He was and is looking for **SUCH.** We then must discover the worth of this to our relationship with Him. Again allow me to define this term **Such?** To worship God in spirit and in truth; reveals the very image and likeness of an eternal God. In the Greek text, this word **Such** is shown to denote character to individuality: Like (as) or such an one; truly this, or of this sort. **We ask ourselves then; of what sort is the God that we serve? Of what is this character comprised? Who is like unto Him?** God has and will make any demand on those who come; which are not consistent with His own character. It is His individuality, which becomes the uniqueness of our relationship with Him. There are none like Him, save those who become yielded to the commands of His Word. The Father first is **SUCH;** and then they which are obedient to the truth, become **SUCH.** In the Old Testament; the Lord revealed Himself as Elohim or El or Elah. These were the first names revealed in Him meaning God. When we look at the noun form of Elah; we see El meaning strength, and Alah which is to bind ones self with an oath or to swear. God then implies His faithfulness even in the first assertions of Himself as God. Because of the need to show men the great and awesome power of God; it is necessary for Gods first acts of creation to be established in concert with His name. God creates the Heavens and Earth in Genesis Chapter One and verse one. His second act of creation is that of animal life (vs.) 21 and then, human life as shown in verses 26 and 27.

Men cannot know what **SUCH** is apart from understanding in some measure, the vastness of the character of HIM; through whom, there is a call for their association and relationship. It is the relationship of men to the sovereign and mighty God that makes them this **SUCH!** It is then, that after the creation of man; God who is revealed in Elohim, reveals Himself as Jehovah-Elohim. *(The Lord God)* This is a revelation of God as the Self existent one or as is clearly shown in Ex. 3:14; He who is who He is, or the I AM. The word Havah from which Jehovah gets its root, points out the merit of His character as the revealer of Himself. So then He is the self-existent One, who reveals Himself. They that are **SUCH,** will become **Such** by the revelation knowledge of the God we serve. It is this revelation of

Jehovah Elohim to Adam; which reveals God as the redeemer from sin. It shows Him as the covenant God, in redeeming Adam through the blood sacrifices which were made. **(God gave them coats of skins)** Gen. 21 It is again seen in His covenant with Israel; to bring them out of the bondages of Egypt. In Ex. 3:13-17 Jehovah as the Redeemer of His people; focuses on the character of God, because of the sin of men and the salvation which He desires to give them. Lev. 19:1-2; *"And the Lord spake unto Moses, saying Speak unto all the congregation of the children of Israel, and say unto them, Ye shall be Holy; for I the Lord thy God am Holy."* Further the Lord shows His judgment and hatred for sin. In Gen. 6:5-7; the Lord shows His complete and utter disapproval of sin. He notes that the wickedness of men was great upon the earth, and *"that every imagination of the thoughts of the hearts of men was only evil continually. It repented the Lord that He had made man in the earth, and it grieved Him at His heart."* And the Lord said *"I will destroy man from the face of the earth: both man and beast, and the creeping thing, and the fowls of the air, for it repenteth me that I have made them."* God is a God of righteousness and desires a relationship of righteousness and faith with His people. Sin is the only reason for separation and annihilation by God. In light of His Holiness, and love of God for mankind: it is the unmerited favor of the sovereign God and His matchless mercy, which are seen in His revelation to men.

There are seven revealed names in the redemptive character of God in the Old Testament. These names bring men into an understanding regarding the care of the Lord, as meeting all the needs and desires of His people. This is a complete care which ranges from salvation and redemption, to the end of all things. It is a faithful keeping of the whole creation, and all of mankind by God: as well as His Love and mercy to us. He is revealed as Jehovah-Jireh, the Lord will provide; (Gen.22:13-14) referring to the promise of God to provide Himself a sacrifice which is pleasing to Himself. **(This is a forerunner to the provision of God in Jesus Christ).** He is Jehovah-Rapha, the Lord that healeth thee, *(Ex. 15:26)*, implying not only physical healing, but also spirit and soul. As Jehovah Nissi, The Lord our Banner, *(Ex. 17:8-15)*; Amalek as a type of war which rages in the flesh, is recognized in the warfare that rages in the life of the believer. It is confirmed in the Word of God by Gal. 5:17; *"for the flesh lusteth against the spirit and the spirit against the flesh; and these two are contrary the one to the other: so that ye cannot do the things that you would."* So then, the Lord our Banner will fight for us and give us strength to do battle against the enemy of our soul. Our victory is due entirely to the help of the Lord. NOTE: it is important to understand the work of God the Father; manifesting a plan of Love and abundant mercy to men who are deserving of death. We have the witness of His wisdom and wondrous power, seen in the unfolding of a will and purpose beyond the thoughts and abilities of men. It is necessary to recognize the gift of God, in learning of Him. He is the only one who could have saved us. The goodness and the severity of the God of all creation is in view: Christ is unveiled in the scripture. Who, but an all powerful and all knowing God, could bring us into this wonderful grace and abiding assurance!!!

This then, is the character of **SUCH** an one, manifest to our hearts by the will of His spirit. We again, begin to discover the treasures of the God who hath called us to receive the purposes of His heart. As Jehovah-Shalom; the **Lord send peace;** or the **Lord our peace**: He reveals the desire of the Lord to remove the stain and sting of sin and death. He loves and saves sinners, but does it only through the blood of sacrifice. All sin is judged through the shedding of blood. Heb. 9:22 declares that; *"Almost all things are by the law purged with blood and without the shedding of blood is no remission."* When He then reveals Himself as Jehovah-ra-ah; **The Lord my Shepherd;** He shows the greatness of His providence, to lead and care for all of His sheep that are in the earth. He is their divine protector and giver of fields to graze in, and water to drink. He assures that there is peace provided by His grace and restoration from the rigors of life. **(Ps.23)** Jehovah-Tsidkenu, the **Lord our Righteousness,** then unveils the joy of having been redeemed from the curse of sin, and established in the righteousness of a faithful God. Jer23:6 states; *"In His days, Judah shall be saved, and Israel shall dwell safely: and this is his name whereby he shall be called, The Lord our Righteousness."* This reference to the future restoration and healing of Israel; then becomes the hope of a nation, for fulfillment of the blessing of a people of His own. The last redemptive name; Jehovah-Shammah, asserts **the abiding presence** of the eternal God with His people. In Exodus 33:14-15, God assures Moses that: *"My presence shall go with thee, and I will give rest, And He said unto him, if thy presence go not with me, carry us not up hence."* Moses is resolved to not do anything apart from the presence and purpose of God. We as believers are compelled to have the same assertive disposition. Without Christ we can do nothing: and yet with God all things shall be possible. Through then, the power of the Spirit of the Lord; we come into a right relationship with Him. We are not only able to enter into this relationship through the Lord Jesus Christ, having been washed in the blood of sacrifice; but to become like the God of our salvation. We are empowered to become Sons that believe on His name. The Apostle John declares this in the first chapter of John the 12th verse. It is now imperative to give our hearts to understanding the purpose and function of the Spirit of God in the fulfilling of the desire of His heart: To reveal the Church, for the whole world to see. This then implies that the body of Christ will be the likeness of the one who died for it. It will be reproduced in a body of believers who have become the mirror image of Christ himself. Christ, who alone has brought us into the liberty of the Spirit of God and been given power to subdue all things in heaven and earth; will first subdue his body **(the Church)** and bring it into full subjection to the will of God the Father by Christ. He will then give it access to power and authority to subdue the whole earth and bring it ordered to the will of Christ.

The first concern is that it is Christ who defeated Satan and destroyed the works of sin and death. The adversary does not recognize any authority that is less than his own. We as men have no authority that is able to subdue him and destroy his works **(Satan's)** in and of our own strength. It is the power of Christ working in us that will defeat him. Yet power is only released by agreement. *(**Where two agree as touching anything**)* Therefore, the Church must first agree with Christ before it can receive power. It is our ability to agree that shows our relationship to Him. In that setting forth of this relationship and coming into agreement with Him; we find that we cannot come into agreement with him without being changed into his image and likeness. Our agreement is not merely the assent of the mind, but the change of heart and walking out of His will in our will that brings His image. His image in us then is born out in the evidence of our character to do even as he does. We become **SUCH.** The church will not only reflect the image, but imbibe and radiate His character.

CHAPTER SEVEN

THE SUCH
(A GENERATION OF JOSHUA'S)

God in this generation has shown a parallel of the Church through the Law of the Old Testament. It is seen in the changing of the leadership and ministry of Moses; and the installing of Joshua as the captain of Israel. We must recognize the consistencies of the changes that were made then, as parallel with the changes which are being made now. Moses had gone as far with the children of Israel, as he could go in leading them to the land of promise. Yet in spite of all that the nation had seen and experienced of the power and holiness of the Lord God; they could not receive the fullness of the inheritance. (**go and possess the land**) In the generation of Moses, they could not go in and possess the land that the Lord God had given them because, "*The word preached did not profit them, not being mixed with faith in them that heard it.*" Heb. 4:2b Israel saw the miraculous intervention of the death angel to destroy their enemy; while they themselves were protected by the blood which was struck upon the lentils of the doorposts of their homes. This being then an awesome testimony of the love and the saving grace of their great God; became a memorial of the tremendous work of salvation for his people. Even when they had received their freedom and were gone out of Egypt; they again witnessed the providence of the Lord God: When their backs were against the sea and the enemy was behind them, to press them and destroy them: God divided the waters and delivered them on dry ground while destroying the host of the Egyptian armies in the waters of the Red Sea. In like manner, there have been many that received the awesome miracles and power of the Mighty God. Many have been healed of various diseases, supernatural deliverance has taken place in the lives of others; yet there has been a vacillation and ambivalence by the people of God to receive His whole purpose and will. This has been the results of the teachings of men. Teachings of denominationalism, sectarianism, and racism, along with occultic mixes of spiritism and the like which, have found their way into the Church. This intervention of men through religion, and new age thinking; have served to be a foundation and catalyst for the negating of the wisdom of God in the Church. In the days of Moses, God was to be the source and supply for the well-being of the nation; yet, in the quest to come into the land of promise; they rather than trust God; began to tempt God. They murmured against His desire and purpose for their lives. In Exodus 16:2; *"The whole congregation of the children of Israel murmured against Moses and Aaron in the wilderness."* They even in their murmur and complaint, thought it best to be in their land of bondage and die having meat to eat; than be there in the wilderness. . . . . .FREE. With no understanding that the same God that brought them out of Egypt; would supply all their needs because of their obedience and Love for HIM; They could not see His provision: meat to eat. **(manna from heaven)** This is the pitiful state that can grip the lives of believers. . . . .selfishness and confusion will cause the flesh to seek only to appease itself at any cost; the end result being spiritual bondage.

Many have been in spiritual bondage because of the compromise of the Word of God in their lives. They would rather sacrifice to their flesh, than allow the sacrifice of Christ for them. The Joshua Generation however, will not be such a people. They are a people of courage and **GREAT FAITH.** They are a warrior like nation of people, who will not compromise the things of the Lord to satisfy themselves. The leadership of their generation will be men and women who love God and will not turn aside from the purpose of the One who called them. They will be strong in spirit and faith: demonstratively loyal and obedient; and undaunted by the influences of the world. They will be men and women of an extreme warrior mentality in the spirit. They will press through in the spirit realm to win battles against the enemy at all costs. This is also, a violent generation psychologically, and there are many who will come off the streets, and out of gangs; members of families which have generationally cursed backgrounds; but have been delivered and saved by the power of the Living God. They will have absolutely no regard for the kingdom of Satan or fear of it. This is a generation that will not walk in the hypocrisies of its fathers, but, will stand in truth and the integrity of the Spirit, to perform the will of the Lord. They will do according to Joshua 1:8; *"This book of the law shall not depart out of thy mouth; but thou shalt mediate therein day and night, that thou mayest observe to do according to all that is written therein: For then thou shalt make thy way prosperous, and then thou shall have good success."* This people of the Lord God will be **SUCH**: They will love the Lord God with a fervent and obedient heart. Because of this love for Him: Jesus said; *"if a man love me, he will keep my words"* in John. 14:23; The Church will be the greatest and most powerful force the world has ever seen in any generation. The strength of this is born out in the prophetic utterance of the day. God is raising up the mantle of the Apostle and the Prophet as never before. We must look at these mantles, and the role they will play in the fulfillment of the purposes of God in this hour, in the next book. In continuing to observe the Joshua's of this generation; we find that God has given a prophetic message to the world regarding His defense of His purpose. It is a message that is clearly seen in three parts and cannot be denied.

The first message as noted in Num. 23:7-10; is a message which stems out of the desire of the heathen world to curse them that had been chosen of the Lord God for His service. Balak the king of Moab has sent for a prophet and seer named Balaam to come and curse the people of the Lord God. In Vs. 7; Balaam takes up a parable and speaks to the king regarding Israel. In Vs. 8, he speaks; *"How shall I curse, whom God hath not cursed? Or how shall I defy, whom the Lord hath not defied?"* There is a witness here to all men, that whatever the Lord hath chosen cannot be defied. We have been chosen as the **SUCH** of this world, to fulfill His will. Then Vs. 9 goes on to say; *"From the top of the rocks, I see Him, and lo the people shall dwell alone, and shall not be reckoned among the nations."* This then, is the acknowledgment that God will separate His people from the world. Thus, according to Vs. 10; *"who can count the dust of Jacob, and the number of the fourth part of Israel?* This a number and kindred and tongue that no man can number. It is again born out of the revelation of the Apostle John; Rev. 7:9; *"After this I beheld, and, lo, a great multitude, which no man can number, of all* nations, and kindreds, and people, and tongues, stood before the throne, and before the Lamb, clothed with white robes, and palms in their hands; Vs. 10; And cried with a loud voice, saying, Salvation to our God which sitteth upon the throne, and unto the Lamb." God has always preserved a people for himself. It is the heart and desire of the Lord to bring the witness and evidence of this great move of the Spirit. Christ will manifest himself in the believer in such a manner and way that it will be visible to the whole world. Those believers will however, be fully separated unto the whole purpose and desire of the Living God.

There has been warfare of the enemy (**Satan**) against the Church; a blatant and extremely hostile attempt to take what God has given and blessed and corrupt it. It is the desire of the enemy to separate the people of the Lord from the purposes of the sovereign Christ. He has fought viciously through the mantle of the false Teacher, to focus the truth of God away from the purpose of God through error. (**strongholds**) God has called His people to separation from the wisdom and opinions of men. This separation is in fact a work of the Spirit of the Lord in exposing the tactics of the Wicked One, to redress this error with revelation knowledge and truth, by the spirit of wisdom in Christ Jesus. The Apostle Paul writes to the church at Ephesus; "*Blessed be the God and Father of our Lord Jesus Christ, who hath blessed us with all spiritual blessings in heavenly places in Christ.*" Eph. 1:3 We are already blessed as the people of the Lord. Because of who Christ is to the Church; there is a necessity to seek out the pleasure and desire of Christ to fulfill His will. Vs. 9 and 10 of the same passage states; "*Having made known unto us the mystery of His will, according to His pleasure which He hath purposed in himself. That in the dispensation of the fullness of times, he might gather together in one all things in Christ; both which are in heaven, and which are on earth; even in Him.*" Therefore we must conclude that the Church, will be completely separated to the purposes of the living Christ and not be prevented by the forces of evil against it. It is the **SUCH** of the Lord, who will come out from among the **world's system and way,** and touch not the unclean thing.

The second message is a prophetic parable as well: Vs. 18 *"Rise up Balak, and hear; hearken unto me, thou son of Zippor: Vs. 19; God is not a man that He should lie; neither the son of man that He should repent: hath He said, and shall He not do it.? Or hath He spoken, and shall He not make it good? Vs. 21; He hath not beheld iniquity in Jacob, neither hath He seen perverseness in Israel: the Lord His God is with him, and the shout of the king is among them."* This message is a message of the justification that God gives to the believer through their faith in His word. As the New Testament parallel is put in place; we recognize the strength of who we have become in Him!!! Therefore being justified by faith, we have peace with God through our Lord Jesus Christ: *"By whom also, we have access by faith into His grace wherein we stand, and rejoice in Hope of the glory of God."* Rom. 5:1-2 The believer then is assured of his place in the promise of Christ as determined in the Word of God. The Lord is not a man that He would lie to His people. It is guaranteed in the Word that we have what GOD himself professed concerning us.

The **SUCH** will not waiver in the knowledge and understanding of His truth. The SUCH will embrace the character and heart of God by His spirit, and not allow the enemy of our soul to rob or steal His promise from us. Often, men vacillate with not knowing the way or manner in which things will be accomplished in their lives. We must merely attend to that for which God has made us responsible. We must believe the report of the Lord. God will never defame His character. To not perform His Word would not only be a defamation of His character; but also, the conclusion of all things. To not perform His word would be catastrophic to the continuing of all things in this world. Since all things are predicated on His word; then, nothing would stand or remain: All would be destroyed. *(Heaven and Earth would pass away).* Mt. 5:18 So then, the thinking of men concerning the greatness of the God we serve, as believers, must be limitless in its certainty... That is, that God in Christ Jesus is not to be thought of in the limitations of men. This can happen through refusal to accept the immutability of His word or by not coming into agreement with His person and character. As the sovereign and vast Creator of the universe; in Him is ability beyond man's limited and finite reason. The **SUCH** are a people whose faith is as absolute, to the faith and reason of Christ, as the immutability of His word. This is the essence of the relationship of the believer, to a Masterful God skilled in relationship, and willing to reveal himself to the hearts of men.

There is also, further prophetic statements, in Vs 22-24: of Numbers 23: God brought them out of Egypt; *"He hath as it were the strength of a unicorn."* (Ox) The thought is compliant with the power of the spirit of the Lord God; which is released to His people to endure in the face of opposition and warfare. Isaiah characterizes it in this fashion: *"No weapon that is formed against thee shall prosper; and every tongue that shall rise against thee, in judgment thou shall condemn. This is the heritage of the servants of the Lord, and their righteousness is of me saith the Lord."* Isa. 54:17 The Lord places great emphasis upon the righteousness of His people. He is very adamant for the relationship of faith and obedience, which shows His character. There have been many times, a veneer and facade in the church, which shows a primness and proper expression; but has not the life or the Spirit that pleases God. All righteousness in men is and should be about who Christ is in them and not about who men are to themselves. It is the very heart and desire of the Lord God, to sustain the courage and strength of His people by establishing a relationship of character through Jesus Christ, which supercedes the thinking and social graces of men. The people of the Lord can and shall endure hardness and vanquish the enemies of the Most High God; and in His infinite wisdom, the Lord puts His character into the spirit of His people. We then become **SUCH: (they who possess the Spirit and character of that which they observe as the rule and conviction of their heart)**. In other words we become like that which rules our spirit. God has never lost a war and is absolute victor in all that He does and will do. With the pronounced blessing of the Lord over the lives of His people; there can be no doubt that the curses and enchantments of the wicked are ineffective to stop the march of the church into the fulfillment of its end time destiny. Num. 23:23; *"Surely there is no enchantment against Jacob and neither is there any divination against Israel; according to this time it shall be said of Jacob and of Israel, what hath God wrought!"* It will be clearly seen in every place; the vast strength and power of a matchless God in the Body of Christ. The Church will have a very demonstrable authority in the earth and will do great exploits for the sake of Jesus Christ. The world will literally be confounded for the awesome feats of the Church. The Church will do miracles of healing and deliverance performed through supernatural works of power through Jesus Christ. Note: it will not be a church which is constructed around one or two individuals who have touched God and seen his glory and begin to work his works, but a body ministry. All those in the body of Christ who see his glory and have been touched by him will begin to walk in power and demonstration of his Spirit. Nothing will be able to withstand the wisdom of the Spirit of God that shall be in us. **(What has God wrought?)** Num.23:24 *"Behold the people shall rise up as a great lion, and lift up himself as a young lion: he shall not lay down until he eat of his prey, and drink the blood of the slain."* The believers shall begin in this day and hour to posses the spoil of the world. There is going to be a great outpouring of the power and anointing of the Holy Ghost in the earth. It will be greater than at any other time in the history of man. It is an anointing of the whole world to bring the end-time harvest of souls and to establish the fullness of the Word of God before all men **(and greater works shall ye do).** It will also bring the church into its greatest prosperity of all time. The wealth and riches of the wicked will be put into the hands of the Holy people of the Lord. The wisdom of men will be challenged and defeated because God must show His word in absolute rule and control. He must show the whole world, the power and authority of His Son in the CHURCH to perform the will of God with dominion and complete privilege.

Now, in the third prophecy of Balaam, Balaam recognizes the desire of the Lord to bless His people with continual blessing. In Numbers 24:1; *"and when Balaam saw that it pleased the Lord to bless Israel, he went not as at other times, to seek for enchantments, but set his face toward the wilderness."* Balaam knew that the true and living God was and is the Lord of all creation and would bless whom he bless and curse whom he would curse. Vs.5; *"How goodly are thy tents, O' Jacob; and thy tabernacles O' Israel!"* This is a statement of the blessing of the people of the Lord that is come, because He has chosen them. We have been chosen in Christ Jesus to inherit the blessing of the Lord, Paul tells the Ephesians of this blessing in Eph. 1:4: *"According as he hath chosen us in Him before the foundation of the world, that we should be holy and without blame before Him in love."* So then we are given the prophetic inheritance of the Sons of God because of our adoption as children in Christ.

The word of the Lord continues with this thought in verses 5 and 6 of Ephesians 1: *"Having predestinated us unto the adoption of children by Jesus Christ to himself, according to the good pleasure of his will, to the praise of the glory of His grace, wherein He has made us accepted in the beloved."* Because of this inheritance, we receive the fullness of the promises that God has for His people. We have goodly places to dwell in; and not only so, goodly tents or dwelling places; but the valleys are spread forth; as gardens by the river's side, and we are compared to trees of lign aloes and cedar trees that are beside the waters. This thought suggests the fertile places for growing productive, fruit bearing trees. Water is absolutely essential to the success and well-being of crops. Also, there is in the cedars, the very best material for building, and lign aloes for the work of healing. This is the supernatural water of the Spirit of God which is indwelling to the believer, and causes him to be fruitful and multiply through the incorruptible seed that is given. 1 Peter 1:22 This prophesy signifies that the seed of our God is in the pouring out of many waters and Jesus is the sower and the one who multiplies the seed sown. Christ in the confrontation with the Samaritan Women is challenged that he has nothing to draw water with. John 4:11. Yet, Jesus only speaks of that which he could give. He knew that it could be drawn through our spirit. A further parallel to this is captured in the story of Agag. Agag represents the world and it's lust and desires. He has operated according to his own will. But, Christ as the Son of God is made higher than the princes of this world and is exalted in his obedience to the will of the Father. *(And his king shall be higher than the king of this world).* *(Agag the pagan of Amalek, See: 1 Sam. 15:9)* and the kingdom of God shall be exalted. This exaltation is first established in the witness of the Lord in bringing Israel out of Egypt to inherit the land of promise. Not only is it a mission of inheritance; but a fulfillment of the prophetic utterance of the Lord concerning all that He would do in the earth through the promise He had given to Abraham. Gen.17:8 *"and I will give unto thee, and to thy seed after thee, the land wherein thou are a stranger, all the land of Canaan, for an everlasting possession; and I will be their God."* This is the parallel for the Church of the Living God, which is in the earth today. The Church is a body of believers which have prophetic utterance and the divine redemption of the Lord Jesus Christ. The Church has been called to inherit the fullness of God in Christ Jesus. The **SUCH** of God is born out in the character of the Church **(he seeketh such; them who look, talk, do in manner, appearance and action what he himself does).**

We note that in the course of scripture; there is the mind of the God of all creation calling forth a mighty people to fulfill His purpose. It is set forth in the work of Jesus Christ at Calvary. It is given in the first book of the Bible, by the divine utterance of the Living God. **(Gen. 3:15)** This speaks of Christ being born into the earth to break the curse of sin and death. It is the Word of God to all mankind. In light of this, it is the purpose of the Lord to give men by His Holy Spirit, the coming events of the future. This is the prophetic wisdom of God to reveal to the hearts of men, the things which will surely come to pass. The **SUCH** are those who are going to walk in the full character of Christ. They are going to be built by the Holy Spirit of God much like a master craftsman would build by design the product they envision. It is an assertive and qualitative work of God to complete in man through his Church what he envisioned and purposed in Adam. Adam was made to worship God and know God in intimacy of relationship that was beyond his initial beginning but because of sin became hidden and lost to him. But in the new man Adam **(Jesus Christ)** what we lost; much more did we gain in him. We will as the church be the full embodiment of Christ himself. Hebrews chapter one verse three declares *"who being the brightness of his glory, and the expressed image of his person, and upholding all things by the word of his power, when he had by himself purged our sins, sat down on the right hand of the majesty on high".* We are going to look like Jesus, speak like Jesus and do what Jesus did; and the glory of

God shall be revealed in us as the whole earth is travailing for the unveiling of the sons of God to God's glory. *"Thanks be to God for his unspeakable gift."* IICor.9:15

Printed in the United States
By Bookmasters